*For David, John
and Holly McGrane
W.M.*

*For Henry
J.H.*

First published 1987 by
Walker Books Ltd
184-192 Drummond Street
London NW1 3HP

Text © 1987 William Mayne
Illustrations © 1987 Jonathan Heale

First printed 1987
Printed and bound by
L.E.G.O., Vicenza, Italy

British Library Cataloguing in Publication Data
Mayne, William
Lamb Shenkin.—(Animal library)
1. Readers—1950-
1. Title II. Heale, Jonathan III. Series
428. 6 PE1119

ISBN 0-7445-0728-6

Lamb Shenkin

Written by
William Mayne

Illustrated by
Jonathan Heale

WALKER BOOKS
LONDON

The first thing Lamb Shenkin ever touches in this world is a drift of snow, so cold, like the North Pole.

His mother has never heard of the North Pole. "No need of that," she says. "Now, my lamb, stand up, be a good fellow, and let your Ma lick you warm."

The first thing that Lamb Shenkin sees in the dark night is the shepherd's lantern bob-bobbing through the falling snow, shepherd coming to see that he was born, how many and what colour.

"Yin," says the shepherd, and that is the first thing Lamb Shenkin hears. "Well done, Mother, he's strong and healthy."

"Maa," says Ma, soft and proud. And now the first thing Lamb Shenkin tastes is his own mother's milk, warm, rich, welcome.

Then he is ready to lie down beside her out of the wind, while she looks at him and smells him until she knows him from all the lambs in the world.

"Well, what else?" says Lamb Shenkin. "Who else could I be?"

Now and then, however, in the snow-lined fields, under the cold skies, he will go to the wrong mother, who does not want him, indeed not at all, and butts him away.

He stands and shouts for Ma, until he finds her. With his tail wagging in the air he dives under her for milk.

When the snow has begun to melt he sits on top of her, a soft, warm place.

When the grass begins to grow short and green he nibbles a little.

One day the shepherd comes with lad and dog. It is a Welsh collie. "Back, back," it says, and makes Lamb Shenkin hop.

All the flock of ewes and lambs goes in the corner of the field, and every lamb is taken away from every Ma.

There is noise. There is shrieking. There is something of a fuss. The dog covers his ears.

The ewes eat the grass calmly. They have heard all this before. They trust the shepherd and the lad, sometimes even the dog.

Each lamb loses his tail, one by one. At Lamb Shenkin's turn the shepherd says, "No, not that one, leave that one. We don't want the tail off him."

When all the lambs go back to their mothers there is more fuss again.

"There, there," says Ma, "they say it doesn't hurt; but is the place sore, Shenkin?"

"They have not cut my tail off, Ma," says Lamb Shenkin. "'Not that one, look,' they said. They don't care for me, and why is that?"

"There will be enquiries," says Ma, but when she goes to ask the shepherd he and the lad and the dog have gone. Glad to see the tail of that old dog, yes.

"I never heard of that before," says Ma. "Always, always, they cut the tails off lambs, specially boy lambs."

"Perhaps," says Lamb Shenkin, "perhaps I am not good enough."

"You're good enough for me," says Ma. "Come to your milk, Shenkin."

A little later in the year Lamb Shenkin begins to climb the walls and run about the next field, naughty. One day he gets out to the road and is nearly trotted down by a horse. Very frightened, he is, thinking it is a steam engine.

"That's a bad one," says the shepherd, when he sees Lamb Shenkin run the whole street all wild and woolly. "That's trouble, now." And he puts Lamb Shenkin in the field again. "I'll have my eye on you, Shenkin," he says.

Lamb Shenkin learns to fight the other lambs, head to head, and all the other lambs have headaches, because Lamb Shenkin is rough, strong and heavy, and has grown horns.

All the lambs are
marked with green
paint, to tell who
their shepherd is. All
except Lamb Shenkin. He is not marked at all.

"Not good enough again," he says, and stands
by himself in the deep grass, quite ashamed.

"I am deeply worried," says Ma. "I shan't be
fit to clip. Things are not as they should be."

Other shepherds come to look at Lamb
Shenkin.

"I think he will never come to anything,
that one," says the first.

"A lot of fuss about nothing," says the second.

"Not worth the trouble," says the third.
They whistle up their dogs and go away.
Ma stamps her foot at them.

Lamb Shenkin wonders what is wrong with him. It makes him wild, and Ma worries why he is a disgrace. She worries more when it is time for all the lambs to go. Every one, except Lamb Shenkin, goes shouting, skipping and nibbling up the hill, down the dale, to the market.

There is no one for Lamb Shenkin to play with. Ma's coat frets away with despair. The other ewes butt Lamb Shenkin severely. "Where are all my playmates?" he asks. "What is wrong with me?"

His shepherd takes him away one day. Lamb Shenkin expects he will be punished for being Lamb Shenkin, the only thing he knows.

"Special treatment, boyo," says the shepherd. He takes Lamb Shenkin to a barn. "We'll see if we can't make something of you."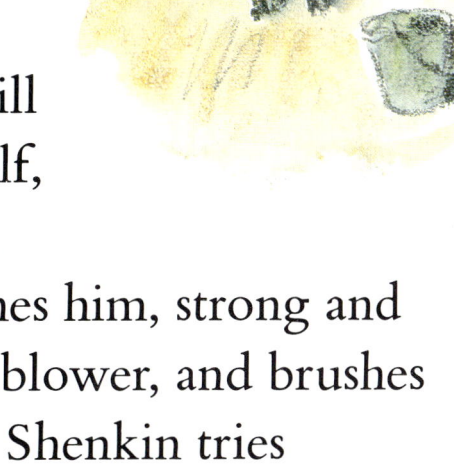

Lamb Shenkin tries to say that if they will tell him what is wrong he will try to be better by himself, out in the field with Ma.

But the shepherd washes him, strong and special, dries him with a blower, and brushes his coat. It tickles. Lamb Shenkin tries to be away.

"You are a bad one," says the shepherd, and calls the dog to help, the lad to hold.

Lamb Shenkin calls for Ma. She is too ashamed to come, see, all this work to make her lamb proper. What will they think of her? Why can't he be ordinary?

Lamb Shenkin is put in a place with straw all night, with hay to eat, and little sheep nuts. In the morning early, when he really wants Ma most of all, and a drink of milk, the shepherd comes again. This time, goodness, he polishes Lamb Shenkin's horns.

"There now," he says, "you could see yourself in them."

"All this," thinks Lamb Shenkin, "because I am not good enough without. Other lambs don't need it."

Off they go in a horse and trap, shepherd, lad, dog and Lamb Shenkin, up the hill and down the dale, to a place with such a lot of sheep, dogs, horses, carts, so many shepherds there can't be so many sheep.

But there are. Lamb Shenkin is looked at, prodded, lifted, paraded; well, you would think they will know him now, next time, and last time as well, at this rate.

In the end a collar goes on him, and a label. Lamb Shenkin thinks it says "Do not be like this boyo."

But when he is home Ma says, "I never did, no, fancy! First prize you have won, best Lamb Shenkin in the world, it says. So don't look so sheepish, Shenkin. All that ignorance they gave you, well, it was just keeping you and saving you for the great show."

Next year see Shenkin, not a lamb any more, but best ram in the world, getting proud too, and quite forgetting which is his Ma, I'm sorry to say.